Illustrations
of
Old Bideford

Volume Five

Peter Christie

Edward Gaskell *publishers*
DEVON

First published 2012
Edward Gaskell *publishers*
The Old Gazette Building
6 Grenville Street
Bideford
Devon
EX39 2EA

isbn (13) 978-1-906769-37-6

Illustrations of Old Bideford
Volume Five

Peter Christie

Typeset, printed and bound by
Lazarus Press
Caddsdown Business Park
Bideford
Devon
EX39 3DX
www.lazaruspress.com

Dedicated to
Gracie

Lazarus Press
DEVON

Contents

Edward Gaskell *publishers*
DEVON

Introduction

In Volume 4 I expressed surprise that I had managed to publish four volumes of *Illustrations of old Bideford* - well here is number five! It may seem exceptional that such a small market town can have a history so well documented by illustrations but I suspect that many similar sized towns could conjure up an equivalent number of pictures. In fact I am now compiling Volume 6 which should appear in 2013. If I decide that this is the final one in the series I intend including an index to all the illustrations. As before I would add that if you have any photographs which might be of interest to fellow-Bidefordians and others then please do contact me on Bideford 473577 or at 9 Kenwith Road, Bideford EX39 3NW.

Photographs have been lent to me by the following people who retain the copyright:

J.Baker	M.Jewell
Bideford Camera Club	M.Martin
Bideford Library	B.Morrish
Bideford town council	North Devon Journal
G.Braddick	North Devon Record Office
J.Brownrigg	North Devon Museum Trust
S.Chappell	P.Paddon
C.Cock	B.Pidgeon
M.Davey	J.Sims
V.Eastman	J.Swain
T.Farley	D.Warmington
D.Gale	Mr & Mrs.Way
B.Harris	J.Webb
T.Hatton	P.Wells
J.Jenn	G.Willett
	C.Wood

Front Cover
This extremely clear shot of the Bridge prior to the 1925 widening shows an early motor lorry belonging to the Bideford Co-operative Society crossing the river. The industrial buildings lining the East-the-Water bank stand out clearly and there is a lot of steam to the left which is possibly a train going to Barnstaple.

Back Cover
Local men of the 4th (later 6th) battalion of the Devonshire Regiment march down Grenville Street around 1910. The man wearing the leopard skin in the fourth row back is Stanley Shortridge (without his bass drum) whilst the man on the extreme right of the second row back is Fred Kivell.

Illustrations of Old Bideford
Volume 5

The Bridge

Above: Any collection of Bideford photographs has to contain shots depicting the Bridge in its 1864-1925 incarnation. The first here was photographed by Archibald J.Coke of Newton Abbot and sold as a tourist memento. The complete absence of any wheeled (or horse) traffic is amazing to us who have grown used to the continuous flows of cars and lorries using it.

Next page: The second is a beautifully composed picture centred on the Bridge which clearly shows the different arch widths but note the railway wagons to the right and the coasting vessel on the East-the-Water mud. Bridge Buildings have yet to be built which dates the shot to before 1882

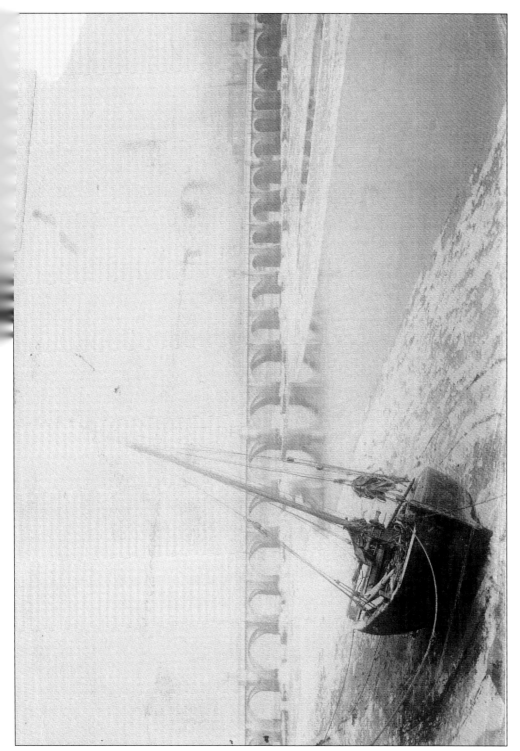

This rather faded shot shows the Torridge covered to a large extent in ice – a situation that occurred most seriously in the Winter of 1894-5. A photograph in Vol. 1 of this series shows the event and I suspect this picture was taken in the same year.

An unusual viewpoint is shown here – with at least 6 horse drawn vehicles present. Careful examination of the shot shows a bare rough wall on the Town Hall corner which suggests the picture dates from around 1904 when the old chemist's shop belonging to Mr.Hogg had been demolished to make way for an extension of the Town Hall.

Above: A very unusual view here taken from a boat. It is looking through one of the arches near the eastern bank – with the iron work on the Bridge shown very clearly.

Next page: This 1920s aerial view of East-the-Water shows the mass of industrial buildings and warehouses well; additionally the railway goods yard has a long line of trucks present – and the different configuration of the sand banks from today is very obvious. Next to the Bridge appears to be a vessel in the throes of construction under a large roof covering.

When the two westernmost arches of the Bridge gave way in January 1968 Bideford was severed in two – and numerous amateur photographers captured the demolition/rebuilding over the next year or so. These two photographs show the demolition of the pier and its subsequent reconstruction, with the wooden templates for the arches in place. The arch on the right is more advanced than the left but note the cantilevers above the arches which have themselves recently had to be strengthened.

Shops

Above: E.J.Tattersill was a grocer who began with one shop in Torrington and ended with four in Bideford – of which he became Mayor over the years 1902-4. He was also chairman of the Bideford & Bristol Steamship Company which ran the s.s.*Devonia*. This shot from 1904 shows the branch in the Market Place, the premises now house a furniture shop.

Next page: This advertising woodcut dates from the end of the nineteenth century and shows that part of Heywood's drapery shop in Grenville Street which now houses an 'Art Deco' shop-cum-store. The figures are deliberately made to appear small to emphasise the grandeur of the building behind them.

This fine portrait of Farleigh's Stores in High Street echoes the photograph in Volume 1 of this series. The wonderfully displayed goods in the window were one of the noted features of this store - which today houses 'New Look'.

This wonderful Edwardian shop front full of jewellery was run by Grimes in the High Street. Happily the frontage survives today with the shop housing Watson's Newsagents. Note the large gas lamp over the doorway which had its illumination reflected off mirrors set in the roof above.

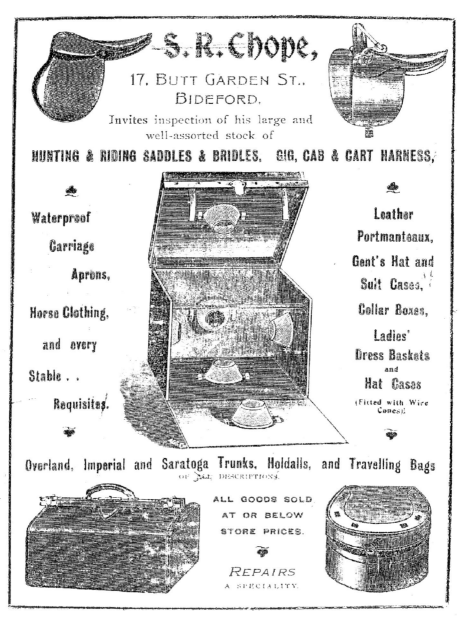

Above: In Volume 2 I had a photograph of Chope's first shop in Buttgarden Street and this pre-World War One advertisement shows some of the goods they sold.

Next page: Chopes in the High Street was Bideford's largest shop for many years following its foundation in 1898 and subsequent growth – but in 2010 it bowed to the twin pressures of on-line shopping and out-of-town malls and the major part of the business closed though it was reopened the following year as M&Co. This photograph dates from 1928 just prior to the demolition of the existing building and its replacement by a more modern shopfront.

Above: The Heavitree Arms at the junction of Mill Street and Lower Gunstone is still in existence today. The name comes from the Heavitree Brewery at Exeter but I am unsure what the date of this shot is – but it was taken at a period when the outsides of public houses were deliberately uninviting owing to pressure from temperance societies.

Previous page: This rather damaged picture shows the staff of Lang's upholstery business in Grenville Street around 1920. The men were, from left to right; ?, ?, Harding, ?, ?, Sid Shute, ?, Mr.Lang, ?, ?. The shop now houses a business selling curios.

Next page: The bookshop of G.W.Fluck stood in High Street where M&Co. now stands. It advertises 'Mudie's Select Library' which was a privately run lending library specialising in light fiction. Famously Diana Dors' original name was Fluck - which was deemed inappropriate for a 1950s glamour queen.

F. R. SCHMIDT,

LADIES',

GENTLEMEN'S

AND CLERICAL

Tailor and Outfitter,

80, HIGH STREET,

—————————— BIDEFORD.

Liveries and .
. . Uniforms

At Lowest Possible Prices.

PRICE LIST & REFERENCES
ON APPLICATION.

With his London and Edinburgh experience
as Practical Tailor and Cutter,
F.R.S. can guarantee
fit, style, comfort and best workmanship.

✳ ✳ C. LANG, ✳ ✳ ✳ ✳ ✳

Boot & Shoe Establishment

64 and 65, Mill Street,

Bideford. ✦ ✦ ✦ ✦

Sole Agent for—

"ROYAL FEODORA" BOOTS & SHOES,
as made for Her Majesty the Queen.

"LOYALTY" BOOTS & SHOES,
as made for T.R.H. the Princess of
Wales and Duchess of York.

Ready and Home-made Boots of every description.   All Repairs neatly executed.

I couldn't resist these
early advertisements.
C.Lang's 'Boot & Shoe
Establishment' is still
recognisable in Mill
Street as the travel agent
adjacent to the Co-op.
A later incarnation is
shown on p.26

J. & H. HEYWOOD,

GENTLEMEN'S COMPLETE OUTFITTERS.

——:o:——

EVERY DESCRIPTION OF CLOTHS IN STOCK AT LOWEST POSSIBLE PRICES.

A thoroughly good Suit for 42s., 50s., 63s.

Also, Trousers from 10s. 6d. to 23s. 6d.

A Splendid Line in WHITE LONG-CLOTH SHIRTS, 3s. 6d.   6 for 20s.

Owing to its narrowness not many photographs seem to have been taken of shops in Mill Street - so this one is quite unusual. 'Lang's Depot for Boots & Shoes' was where the First Choice shop is today and appears in an earlier incarnation on p.25. I would give the date as the 1950s.

Our Speciality.

Smart MILLINERY

AT

Moderate Prices.

WE carry all through the season a large stock of the Latest Novelties in Chiffon Hats and Toques, Fancy and Plain Chip and Crinoline Hats.

If you have any special style you fancy, we shall be pleased to copy it for you.

PRICE RIGHT.

STYLE RIGHT.

QUALITY RIGHT.

WALTER H. CHOPE, High Street, **Bideford.**

Readers of my previous volumes will recall my affection for the ornate bill heads of Bideford businesses past so I couldn't resist including these two. Chopes only disappeared in 2010 though Prowse & Sons closed some time ago. The latter's 1912 bill was sent to H.Ascott who kept the New Inn for many years.

Above: Bideford Pannier Market sometime in the 1960s with real panniers to the fore. The walls are strangely empty but there seems to have been plenty of customers.

Next page: A fine photograph of part of Mill Street in the early 1970s when Nicklin's music shop is seen in the centre with Cording's clothes outlet to the left in the shop that now houses a charity shop.

Above: In Vol.2 I showed a shot of this building in Allhalland Street when it sold ice-cream and boasted of being the smallest shop in town. Here is another of this eccentric little shop with its owner clearly indicating its narrowness. In the 1960s it became a sauna bath connected to Wynne Olley's hairdressing salon on the Quay (next to Mr.Chips). Today the building is merely the entrance to flats in the main block above.

This is another of the many small corner shops that have now disappeared owing to the onward march of the supermarkets. Up until a few years ago it stood at the junction of Torrington Lane and Torridge Mount and was, for many years, run by the Beer family. As with so many of these small outlets it has been converted into housing..

Above: 'Timothy Whites' was a fairly old fashioned 'houseware' shop that had branches in many British towns - including High Street in Bideford, as shown in this early 1970s photograph. The frontage has gone being replaced by Boots and now the Co-operative Pharmacy.

Next page: This building is still instantly recognizable today as the Bank coffee shop in High Street but here from the early 1970s we see it in its initial form as the Midland Bank. The bank itself has also changed its name to the HSBC and is to be found today on the Quay.

Above: On p.29 Cordings clothing shop appears and here we see a later incarnation from December 1975. The building is still recognisable today housing 'Ian Snow' Next door used to be the 'Kingsbury' fishmonger's shop.

Next page: Taken in March 1976 Holman, Ham & Co were chemists in the shop at the left hand junction of the Quay and High Street. The reference to 'Photographic Supplies' connects the shop to a strange 'greenhouse' like structure that once stood on the building's roof which was used as a naturally lit early photographic studio.

Grenville Street is one of those 'working' streets that, in my experience, has rarely been photographed so it was nice to come across this shot. Taken in October 1976 it shows the old grocery shop of J.W.Baker - a shop that has been lying empty and derelict for many years now.

Above: This shop in Buttgarden Street opposite Tower Street is no longer a retail outlet but the 'Mace' franchise pictured here was the successor to Dingle's grocery store. The photograph dates from October 1976 - and note the long vanished Wrigley's chewing gum machines on the wall.

Three shops pictured in Buttgarden Street around 1976 all of which have now ceased trading. T.John's saddlery is on the right, the Withypot pottery is in the centre with Hamlyn's the decorators on the left in a beautiful 'Arts and Crafts' house.

This little corner of Jubilee Square has greatly changed since this shot was taken in October 1977. The antique shop was run by the gentlemanly Mr.Sluman whilst next door was the Ponderosa Snack Bar - both of which have been converted into private houses. Recent research shows the cafe building to be one of the oldest surviving structures in the town.

These two High Street shops just above the Grenville Street junction were photographed in January 1978. Petherick's fishing tackle shop has been replaced by
Dragon Tattoos with Chandler's Antiques next door becoming a domestic building.

Above: Corner shops were once very common but now they are a threatened species. This one stood on the corner between Old Town and Meddon Street and has, within the last few years, been changed from an off-licence to private accommodation. The picture was taken in August 1978.

Next page: The buildings in this 1970s photograph are easily recognisable as they still stand on the Quay but of the five businesses shown only Wimpy is still there today. What older readers may recall is the glass fronted map in the middle of the photograph where 'attractions' lit up when a button was pushed.

The antique dealing firm of Collins still exists in Bideford but not in this building which is now a private house. Established in the High Street for many years its very ornate ship's figurehead and giant 'bellows' were all iconic objects in the street scene until the business closed, to later re-open on the Pill. This particular shot dates from March 1975.

Above: The publisher of this book, Edward Gaskell, started business in Bideford as a bookseller and here is his shop in Grenville Street in 1994 – with its 'illegal' pavement display of wares! In October of that year he vacated the premises and I took them over for the next 14 years running them as a secondhand record/book shop – until the internet made trading conditions too difficult.

Buildings

Above: In previous volumes I have included shots of the various events staged to raise funds for the town's hospital and this is another where the Mayor and council are marching up Meddon Street around 1905. The Workhouse behind them was rarely photographed and I have never previously seen the ventilator on the roof of the building – a lucky inclusion by the photographer.

The Bible Christians opened their Silver Street chapel in 1844 enlarging it in 1866. In 1907 they joined the Wesleyan Methodists and this chapel went on to become in turn a glove factory, a snooker hall, and a night club before being demolished in 2004 and replaced by housing.

Above: The 'Old Ring of Bells' public house stood in Honestone Street near where it joins the Market Square and was typical of the small inns that were to be found all over Bideford in the late nineteenth and early twentieth century. Most like this one have now disappeared reflecting changes in drinking habits.

Next page: This building pictured around 1920 is in Bridgeland Street and sits between 'Dr.Candler's house' to the left and The Red House to the right. It was probably built around1750 and had the then fashionable stucco plaster applied around sixty years later – a good example of how buildings are updated to meet changing fashions.

48

Above: This view won't be identifiable by many today. It shows the right hand side of Chingswell Street when a large house known as 'North View' with its imposing front wall stood on the site. This was taken down and replaced with new houses along both this frontage and along the Strand.

Previous page: The Joiner's Arms in the Market Place is one of the most atmospheric pubs in Bideford and during the Edwardian period it housed a very posh looking dining room in the building that still extends to its right. This postcard shows the interior – when it was known as Vicary's Dining Room.

Next page: The Art School on the Quay was built in 1884 and appears here with bunting and ornamental leaves possibly celebrating Queen Victoria's Diamond Jubilee. I always smile when I see the large commemorative plaque on its wall where the Mayor's name dwarfs that of the architect.

Above: Barnstaple Street was a very narrow entrance to the town until the town council widened it in the 1920s. This shot shows the nearly completed widening and the new road surface that accompanied it.

Previous page: Moreton House is now virtually engulfed by housing but before it became part of the old Grenville College it was a large private estate with its own ornately 'rustic' gatehouses – including this one which is thought to have been near where Moreton Park Road enters Abbotsham Road today.

Above: I have noted before that photographs of the Pannier Market are surprisingly rare so I was pleased to see this one. It shows one of the many cage-bird exhibitions held in the Market with the very distinctive roof clearly shown. I would date it to around 1900.

Next page: The Quay when it still had three out of four adjoining pubs. Today only the King's Arms survives although the Old Ship Tavern is still recognisable in its present incarnation as Mr.Chips.

55

Allhalland Street in the 1920s. Phillips Library was a lending library which operated on an annual fee basis – and next to it is J.Cottle's café offering 'Hot and Cold Luncheons'. On the right hand side is the tiny shop shown on p.30 and beyond that is C.Passmore's upholstery business.

Coldharbour and Gunstone have rarely been photographed in my experience so this one is quite a rarity. It shows the top of Coldharbour in the 1920s when it seems all the cottages were lime washed and Bideford really was 'The little white town'.

West Bank School was founded in Lansdowne Terrace in 1896 as a private secondary school before eventually occupying a large building at Belvoir Hill. It moved in 1955 to Sidmouth and its premises were taken over by Grenville College. This photograph shows one of the boarder's bedrooms in the 1930s which looks rather Spartan I have to say.

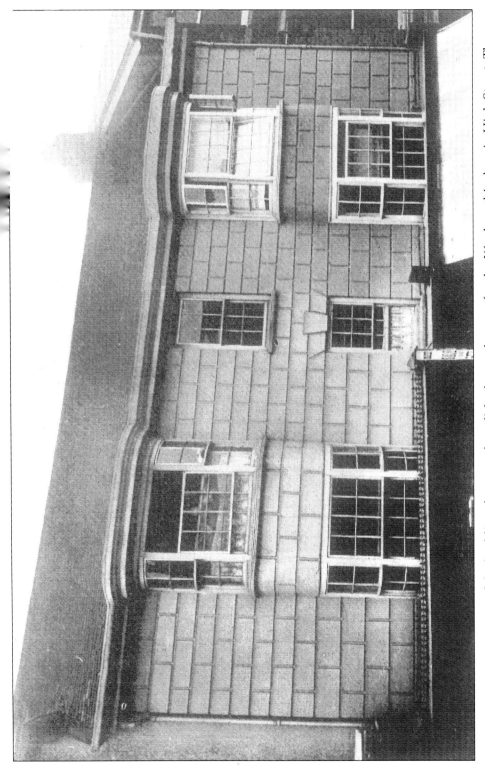

This is the top two storeys of the building that was demolished to make way for the Woolworth's shop in High Street. The photograph dates from around 1924 so probably there are very few alive who can remember this view.

Above: This odd little building which features in many photographs on the Quay was the main town bandstand. Development work saw it being shifted to a garden at Westward Ho! where it was called the Octagon and from here it went into storage at the district council depot in Torrington - where, sadly, the ornamental slates were stolen and so it disappeared.

Next page: Heard's garage on the Quay with its 'new showrooms' displays both the odd copper cupola and the pavement based petrol pumps as well. The now green cupola is a much loved part of the scenery of Bideford though the garage has now been replaced by a convenience store with flats over it.

GARAGE
GARAGE
HEARD BROTHERS, LTD
HEARD BROTHERS LIMITED
ENGINEERS
SERVICE
AUTOMOBILE

This was the 1934 architect's drawing for the proposed new Bideford Grammar School in Abbotsham Road, It was eventually built to a slightly different set of plans in 1935 - and was demolished in 2010 to make way for the futuristic Bideford College under my old student Veronica Matthews..

This old shoe shop stood at the northern end of Mill Street. The building was completely rebuilt being turned into a fish and chip shop which still operates today under the name of 'Trawlers'.

The fairly dark shot shows Sunnyside at East-the-Water in the 1950s before the allotments in front were built over. The terrace was developed in the 1860s for the many industrial workers who lived this side of the river with its name coming from the fact that it was south facing and thus very sunny.

The much loved 'Rose of Torridge' cafe began life as a merchant's house directly overlooking the river in 1626. In this shot from April 1956 it is clear how the pavement and roadway have been built up over the years - until today one has to step down into its current incarnation as the 'Mr Chips' shop.

Ursuline Convent, Bideford.

The Ursuline convent, or the later Stella Maris, has now been converted into a new Housing Association development. The striking conservatory has now gone but the building is still easily recognisable today

This family shot shows members of the Grant family but I have included it here for the way it records the odd little shelter behind them on a site now occupied by the undistinguished Post Office – a building not often photographed in my experience.

Above: Bridgeland Street was a building project by the Bridge Trust which in the last decade of the seventeenth century set out plans for a very wide and grand street of merchants' houses. This shot from December 1964 shows how they achieved it - even if the houses had become shops by then.

Next page: Bideford taken from Raleigh Hill looking across the Kenwith Valley before the two lakes were dug and the whole area became part of a massive flood relief scheme designed to permanently halt flooding in the Northam Road area.

Industry

Above: This cheery looking group of stevedores was pictured in the mid-1950s on Bideford Quay hauling on ropes which presumably were attached to a vessel just out of view. The old toilet block behind them is clear - but where are all today's cars?

Next page: This striking photograph from around 1860-70 shows the Ching family. They were, back row, left to right; Robert, Bryant, John, Richard, James, Hugh, Mary (wife of John). Front row; Maria, Elizabeth, Grace, Mary and Sarah. Looking out of the window is John and Mary's son. I have included it as Bryant (1814-1903) was the owner of a pottery at Hallsannery and later one at Torrington Lane, East-the-Water – where, unfortunately, he went bankrupt in 1867.

Above: Wickham's was a long established wine merchant based on the corner of High and Grenville Street. This picture shows employees loading beer casks from the Market Place section of their premises. From left to right the men were; F.Branch, W.Hanwright, R.Mitchell, J.Sawyer, H.Jeffery and L.Gutsell.

Previous page: This fine study of one of Bideford's fishing boats unloading alongside the Quay dates from the 1930s – and the event clearly attracted onlookers as the vessels still do today.

Next page: This photograph shows workers at Bideford's 'Pot Black' factory, which produced snooker tables, in January 1982. It was taken to mark the expansion of the firm after a record year during which Steve Davis was hired to endorse their products. The people in the shot are (left to right) Mike Daden, Margaret Plows and Judy Pangborn.

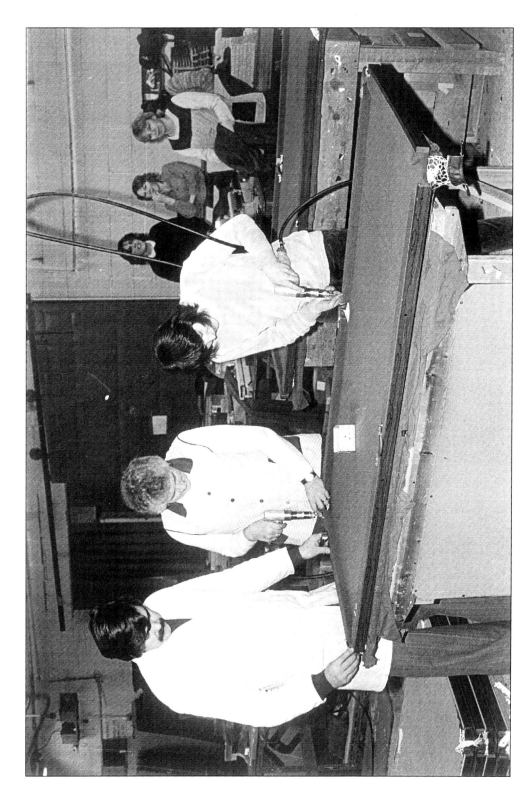

Above: Part of Bank End, where today's Riverbank House stands, was used as the Bideford Shipyard and here we see the area before it was demolished.

Next page: This photograph from April 1984 shows cutting edge computer technology in the form of an electronic organ. Produced after 10 years of research by Wyvern Organs of Bideford the firm were hoping to go into full-time production at their factory in the old East-the-Water Primary School in the town. The photograph shows electronics engineer Dave Chorlton checking some of the 500 microchips in the instrument.

Queen Street once housed a bakery and in 1986 the 'Bakehouse' project was established in this building. Run by Sophie Brown for the Manpower Services Commission it provided cheap start-up units for local would-be entrepreneurs. By February when the photograph of Jenny Urbanowicz's café in the building was taken it housed a potter, woodworker, model maker and sculptor. Since then it has been refurbished again and changed into flats.

David Savage a noted furniture designer is seen here with one of his hand-crafted chairs at his Bideford workshop at Westcombe in September 1987. After studying at Oxford and the Royal College of Art he moved to Bideford in 1984 where he established himself as one of the country's best woodworkers. He is now based in Shebbear.

Transport

In Vol.2 I showed a boat under construction at the Bank End shipbuilding yard and gave a little of the site's history. Here from May 1966 is a clear view of the *Isle of Gigha* alongside Bideford Quay, another of the vessels built at the yard.

Here are two more of Tom Farley's 1950s photographs of shipping at Bideford. The above shows the *Stan Woolaway* which was designed to collect gravel from the bed of the Bristol Channel – but which sank in March 1967. The second shows the *Activity* of London, a small coaster with what looks like a cargo of wood.

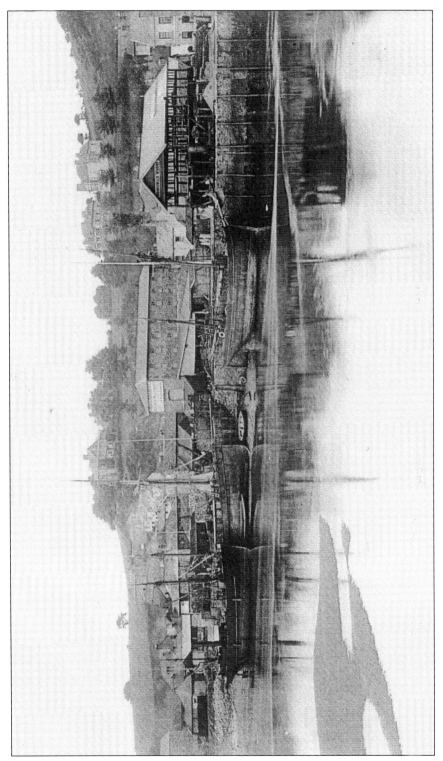

This atmospheric view of the East-the-Water wharfside dates from the early twentieth century and shows a fine selection of wooden vessels with a few large detached houses in the background. At this date water hoses were used to disperse the mud along the quayside which has now become such a feature of the area.

A close up of the previous picture some decades later showing the Ravensdale of Guernsey probably discharging building materials.

Bideford railway station employed quite a few people and here are two shots of them from around 1919. The first shows the station master and booking clerk sitting in front of various porters and other staff. The second shows some of the shunting and office staff and was taken in the yard that now houses Ethelwynne Brown Close. In the back row, from left to right, are Bending, H.Harraway, Bennett. Front row, Easterbrook, Wesley and Bishop.

The bridge carrying Barnstaple Street across the old railway track is shown well here and I have included it as it shows a fine selection of London & South West Railway rolling stock on the right in what was the goods yard – now covered by the houses of Ethelwynne Brown Close.

Above: This railway man with his wonderful sideburns was pictured on the steps of one of the signal boxes at Bideford. Notice his all-important watch and chain for timekeeping. It was taken around 1900 by a keen local amateur Herbert Cooler.

Next page: A later photograph shows the locomotive No.34065 Hurricane coming in to the Bideford Down platform sometime in the early 1960s.

In the last volume I wrote that no book on old Bideford would be complete without a photograph of the Bideford, Westward Ho! and Appledore railway so here are two. The first is a charming shot of the engine and carriage(s) on the Quay possibly on a Regatta Day given the crowds looking over the river. The second, rather faded, shot shows the back of one of the carriages with a group of men in boaters and caps enjoying the views. Note the permanent steps – clearly platforms weren't very high.

BIDEFORD
MOTOR WORKS
EAST - THE - WATER,

(Incorporating Herniman's Carriage Works).

ANY MAKE OF CAR SUPPLIED
AND
FIRST-CLASS BODIES BUILT TO ORDER.

N. DEVON AGENTS for Maudslay, Swift & Ford Cars

17 H.P. MAUDSLAY TORPEDO PHAETON.

One of our Fleet of Hire Cars.

Large Garage. ✿ Well equipped Repair Shop.
Estimates given for all Work.
Leading Makes of Tyres and Accessories Stocked.

Above: A welcome cup of tea dispensed from an odd-looking cupboard-cum-luggage box sometime around the 1920s. The photograph shows Vernon Cock on the left and Leonard Cock and Mrs.Hopcraft on the right. The Cock family were prominent builders in Bideford with John Cock being Mayor in 1905-6.

Previous page: The Bideford Motor Works at East-the-Water had this advertisement in 1913 offering their 'Torpedo Phaeton' hire car and their offer of 'built to order' car bodies – and whatever happened to Maudslay and Swift cars?

Next page: At Easter 1909 the Lord and Lady Mayoress of London visited Bideford and created huge excitement in town. Massive crowds collected on the Quay to greet them – as shown in this photograph. At the rear is one of the engines of the Bideford, Westward Ho! and Appledore Railway with a conductor standing at the front who, unless I am mistaken, appears to be a black man – one of the very first to live in Bideford.

Above: This photograph was taken from Jubilee Square looking out towards the river. The petrol pump to the right was connected to Heard's Garage which was to the left. From the style of the cars and the size of the trees I would date the picture to the 1930s.

Next page: These wonderful Sentinel Steam Wagons were photographed at Clarence Wharf, East-the-Water in 1938 when they were involved in the unloading of the timber boat in the background. The Devon Trading Co.Ltd. later became RGB which is still operating today.

Above: A very solid looking omnibus crosses Bideford Bridge on its way to Barnstaple with a horse and cart nearly keeping up with it behind! The solid-tyred and split-screen 'bus does not look as comfortable as today's 'buses but what a splendid vehicle.

Next page: This fine shot of a later Southern National bus was taken in town, note the destination board showing Landcross and Littleham – not to mention the advertisement for G.F.Truscott of High Street, Bideford. This particular vehicle would have been garaged at the depot shown on p.95

Next to the Bank End shipbuilding yard mentioned on p.75 was the depot of the Southern National bus company. Now covered with a housing estate the yard is shown here complete with a good selection of single and double-decker buses.

This fine study of an old style stagecoach plus a charabanc was pictured outside the New Inn around 1906. The former was possibly on its way to Clovelly which was a popular tourist destination even then. The New Inn has recently been refurbished into a number of apartments.

This photograph dates from around 1937 and was taken at Bull Hill. It shows Mr.Bissett and his magnificently turned out horse prior to going to the Bideford Horse Show. The small decorated butt that the horse is pulling was built by G.Violet & Sons of Torridge Hill.

Above: Readers of a certain age will certainly remember the Cycling Proficiency Trust which was a genuine rite of passage for many. Once you had passed you could take part in events like this 'Cycle Rally' being held at Bideford Secondary Modern (Geneva School) in May 1964 – even if Bideford wasn't designed to make cycling easy!

Previous page: Bideford is full of cars today so this photograph is intriguing. It shows the last horse drawn milk cart in the town in Victoria Grove – with no cars present at all. I am unsure of the date but would guess it to be the 1960s.

Council

Above: In Volume 1 I used a photograph showing the municipal procession marching up Meddon Street past the Hospital (recently demolished). This was on 'Hospital Day' when the whole town turned out to raise funds for the everyday expenses of that institution. The Mayor in the centre of the group is Dr.Edwin Toye who was in office in 1925.

Next page: The Bideford, Northam and District Joint Fire Committee is shown here at the opening of their new Fire Station at Old Town on 21st December 1928 – which was the last remaining section of the Old Town Boys School which, ironically, burnt down in 1926. The engine was known as the *Grenville* with Chief Officer Charles Morris driving it.

King George V celebrated the Silver Jubilee of his reign in May 1935 and the town council assembled in front of the Town Hall to be photographed as part of the events staged to mark the occasion. The Mayor was W.E.Ellis and the vicar the Reverend W.Manning with the mace carrying Beadles at the sides.

These are said to be the council's Victoria Park gardeners pictured in the interwar years. For a long time the Park was famous for its flower beds and greenhouses but things have changed a lot – not least a decrease in the number of men working on the site!

Above: During the Second World War four Mayors filled the office: H.Greenwood, J.Bright, B.Braddick and J.Sharley. The latter is shown here outside a railway carriage.

Previous page: Every year the council chooses a new Mayor and this photograph from 1948 shows Councillor F.T.Upton newly decked out in his robes addressing his fellow councillors in the Town Hall room now used by Torridge District Council.

Next page: The Victorian sounding Poor Law Guardians who ran the old workhouse/parish relief system which looked after the elderly and poor are shown here in the Town Hall at their final meeting on 22 June 1948 just prior to the start of the National Health Service. The Reverend H.C.S.Muller of Appledore is the chairman.

In Volume 3 I published a picture of the Mayor's Parade in May 1956. Here is another one from the same year with a youth band marching up into St.Mary's church to celebrate the occasion.

Above: Another of these 'Mayor's Sunday' shots this one dating from 1961. Although dark I have included it for the long disappeared shops behind the band who were marching down High Street.

Previous page: As part of the day the councillors, led by their Town Crier and Beadles marched along the Quay behind the band.

Above: The Andrew Dole Charity is still in being in Bideford some 450 years after it was set up. In the 1960s the council became involved in distributing loaves of bread to the 'needy' and here from 1967 we see the Mayor and Mayoress Mrs.Vivian Patt and Mrs.L.B.Galliford handing out bread in the Town Hall.

Previous page: The old pre-1974 borough council was able to honour leading citizens by making them 'Freemen of the Borough' and here from March 1972 we see Mayor Pat Hughes presenting commemorative scrolls to four new 'Freemen' – Harold Blackmore, Colonel R.Birdwood, Sir Michael Ansell and Dr.I.Hewetson.

Next page: In 1991 David Brenton was elected Mayor and during his year in office the Landmark Trust who run Lundy decided to move their shore-based headquarters to the town. Here we see councillor Brenton clutching a Bideford 'mug' inspecting the new display board on the Quay with its advertisements about the m.s.*Oldenburg* – which is still in service today.

War Time

Above: This group of British Legion men was photographed outside of the old Bideford Building Society on the Quay sometime in the 1930s. They are carrying wreaths and are wearing their medals – and only one man is hatless. The Legion's HQ was in New Street for many years.

Next page: This fascinating photograph dates from 1926 and shows the Bideford Territorials and local Red Cross nurses on a 'joint exercise' outside the former's Drill Hall on the Pill - which for the duration of the exercise had been converted into a 'casualty ward'. The gentleman on the stretcher to the left is William Piper.

In volumes 3 and 4 I featured photographs of Bideford Home Guard drawn from the collection of William Pascoe and here is another which shows Lt.Pascoe leading his squad along the Quay. The men appear to be very young and I suspect this was a group of trainees.

Above: This rather bizarre photograph appeared in the Bideford Gazette for 15 August 1939 and shows members of the town Air Raid Precaution squad in a very unconvincing 'house' preparing to withstand a gas attack – a very real fear which luckily never became a reality.

Next page: This photograph shows what the trainees were turned into – men of soldierly bearing who clearly would have put up a stiff defence had the Nazis invaded. This photograph shows 'D' (Artillery) Company marching along the Quay to a church service in St.Mary's.

Evacuees and their children were housed in large numbers in Bideford (some 2300 in 1941) and to help bring some normality to their lives a nursery school was set up behind the Methodist chapel in Bridge Street, and this photograph shows some of the children who were taught there – with 3 of their teachers also in the shot.

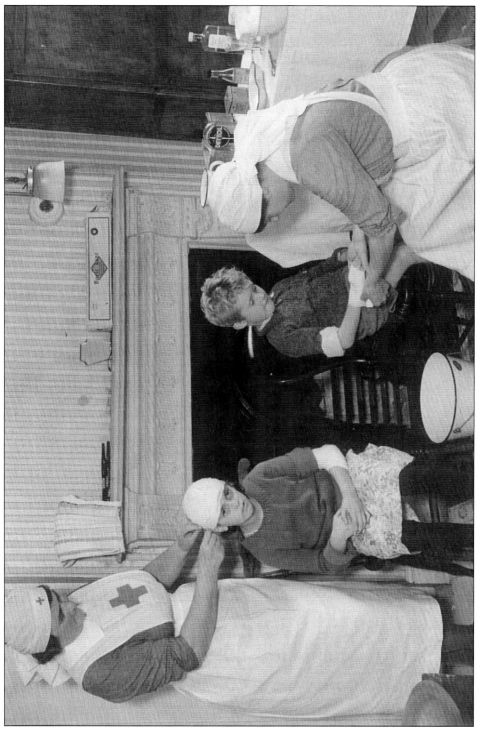

In previous volumes I have published photographs showing wartime refugees and evacuees who settled in Bideford and here is another showing two young 'patients' (whether real or pretend I am unsure) being treated by local Red Cross nurses. Carefully posed these photographs were used as propaganda shots to show Bideford was coping.

Above: In addition to evacuees Bideford played host to people displaced from Europe who had fled Hitler. Housed on sites in Clovelly Road the residents had time to prepare these ornate paintings on concrete slabs recording the pride in their home countries.

Next page: Another group hosted by Bideford was made up of U.S. troops who were housed in local camps and billeted with local families - inevitably there were some 'G.I. brides'. This photograph shows the marriage at St. Mary's of Joan Williams and Robert Terhune with their bridesmaid Marjorie Lucket; her brother Frank Lucket (the sailor) plus Florence, the bride's mother. The soldier is unidentified.

This VE Day party group was snapped in Royston Road and consisted of back row, left to right, David Parkyn, Noel Branch, Brian Harris, John Mugridge, Ron Jones (head out of shot!). Middle row; Maurice Jewell, douglas Fisher, Michael Mugridge, Ron Branch, Tony Harris, John Cox. Front row; ?,?,?, Margaret Cox. ?,?.

Above: Another shot of Mayor Sharley taken at a May 1945 VE (Victory in Europe) Day party held at Sentry Corner.

Previous page: Following the Second World War the Territorial Army became ever more important in terms of supplying back-up manpower to the Regular Army. He is the Bideford TA team who won the local proficiency cup in June 1952 seen with their gun on the Pill.

Sport & Entertainment

Above: Bideford Carnival has had its ups and downs over the years but luckily photographers have always been assiduous in recording the various floats and walking entries as these pictures show. The first dates from the 1920s and shows a horse-drawn float on the Pill bearing the banner 'Hospital's Harvest' which records how the Carnival began – to raise funds for the hospital in Meddon Street. The five ladies would have been using their baskets to collect cash donations.

Next page: The second one also dates from the 1920s and shows a selection of locals dressed as 'foreigners' on a car bearing flags – even if the ones draped over the back wheels do not look very safe.

Bidefordians have always liked a historical pageant and in June 1927 they held a very successful one which featured many townspeople donning their interpretations of historical costume as shown in these two photographs. The first features 'Eliza-bethan' gentlemen and ladies and even Bideford's 'Red Indian' on the left. The second was taken at the Sports Ground with Elliott's old garage building in the background

One of the high points of the day was the arrival of a 'captured Spanish galleon'. The superstructure of this had been built around a local sand barge supplied by P.K.Harris, shipbuilder of Appledore. Constructed in just 3 weeks by W.Jordan of Westward Ho! it was extremely convincing – as can be seen from this photograph.

Next page: One of the most important elements of the Carnival are the onlookers and here from 1947 we see a crowd gathered to wait for the procession outside 'Pullars of Perth' shop on the corner of the Quay and Bridgeland Street. The shop has long gone being replaced by the concrete horror of what is now the 'Britannia' building.

East-the-Water used to elect its own Carnival Queen and here from 1957 we see her and her attendants at Barton Tors. From left to right they were; ?, Caroline Bromwell, ?, Lucinda Moyse, Angela Mitchell (standing). ?, The 'Queen' Valerie Bromwell with Pat Thomas sitting in front, ?.

A later 'Queen' pictured in August 1964. This was taken in the old Cattle Market with the small 'kiosks' evident in the picture.

Another one from the same 1964 Carnival shows the local St.John Ambulance Brigade and their then very topical 'Space craft' float.

Not all carnivals have gone smoothly as this one from the 1980s shows. It co-incided with a very high tide in the River Torridge and led to the scene of flooding seen here – a not uncommon occurrence it has to be said.

Above: The Silver Jubilee of George V in May 1935 was marked in Bideford by a day of celebrations – which began at 7 a.m. (!) when this group of local dignitaries gathered on the Pill to raise a toast to the King.

Next page: As part of the Jubilee celebrations Bideford erected an arch of evergreen boughs from the Town Hall to Bridge Buildings – and here it is with the Town Band marching underneath. Such arches were a common feature whenever the town wanted to celebrate an event.

Another part of the day was given over to a 'Rainbow Pageant' in the Sports Ground. The first photograph shows the opening speeches – with the Mayor W.E.Ellis, Mayoress and Town Clerk standing in front of a mass of children representing the different nations of the Empire. Some of these are shown in close up in the next photograph – with members of the local Boy Scouts, Girl Guides, St.John Ambulance Brigade and Church Lads Brigade all present along with 'Britannia.'

The number of children present is shown well in this shot which I think shows World War One veterans marching on to the field.

This shot shows the proclamation of the new King, George VI, in 1937. The town hall has a display of bunting and greenery and there appears to be a ceremonial mounted 'herald' in the picture.

This large group consisted of members of the Bideford Amateur Athletics Club on a day out at Braunton Burrows on Good Friday 1907. It is recorded that some 83 members were in the group – some 70 of whom played in a football match on the sands! Many of the boys are wearing Eton collars whilst the older men all boast waistcoats and moustaches of varying lengths.

Above: In previous volumes I have printed photographs of various street parties held to mark the Queen's Silver Jubilee in 1977. This is another one taken in Geneva Place with the collection of green boughs across the road being a nod back to the earlier and much larger ones as shown on page 135.

Next page: The Bideford Amateur Athletics Club is one of the town's two sports/rowing clubs and this photograph shows both Junior and Senior Crews in 1910. The moustachioed gentleman sitting to the right of the cups was Vernon Boyle a noted collector of historical material and author.

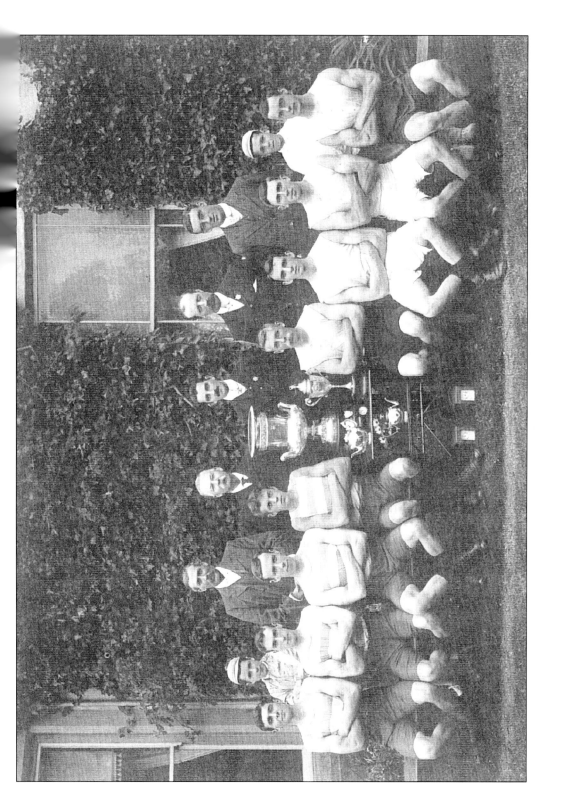

141

A later group shot shows the BAAC 'Junior Champions of the West of England' crew from 1936 proudly posed in front of the silverware they brought back to the club..

Bideford's two rowing clubs have a long and distinguished history yet for many years the sport was restricted to men, but women decided to set up their own team in the mid-1930s and here they are pictured around 1937 on the Pill. From left to right they were; Moore, Joan Manning, ?, ?, ?, Louise Dymond, Sheila Hutchinson, Mary Burton, Satchwell, Elizabeth Deubler.

This crowd was gathered along the river bank sometime in the early 1930s to watch the Regatta races. The sloping bank they are sitting on disappeared when the new Riverbank car park and Landivisiau Walk were constructed in 1991.

Another picture of the crowds gathered on the Quay on a Regatta Day in the 1930s. The vessels tied up along the harbour wall provided a useful series of floating grandstands.

Above: The scene is the Bideford Sports Ground and the event was the first ever go-kart race meeting held in July 1971. Put on by the town's Round Table the eight race meeting raised some £200 for local charities. Each race consisted of 5 laps around the football pitch with the fastest time being recorded by D.Cloke at 2 minutes 41 seconds. A woman-only race was won by Christine Cording after an exciting last minute driving duel.

Previous page: This was the Bideford Amateur Football Club in November 1952 during a good season. In the back row, from left to right are; ?, Bill Barber, Ron Mills, Ernie Butler, Derek Bidgway, G.Langdon, Steve Bowden. Front row; D.Kitto, Roy Cann, Bruce Hocking, Richard Hocking, Leonard Williams. Roy went on to become a noted local postcard collector and I have featured some of his collection in my books.

Next page: Cricket has always been a popular sport in the town and pictured here is the Bideford Grammar School Old Boy's team of 1952 posing on the Abbotsham Road playing fields.

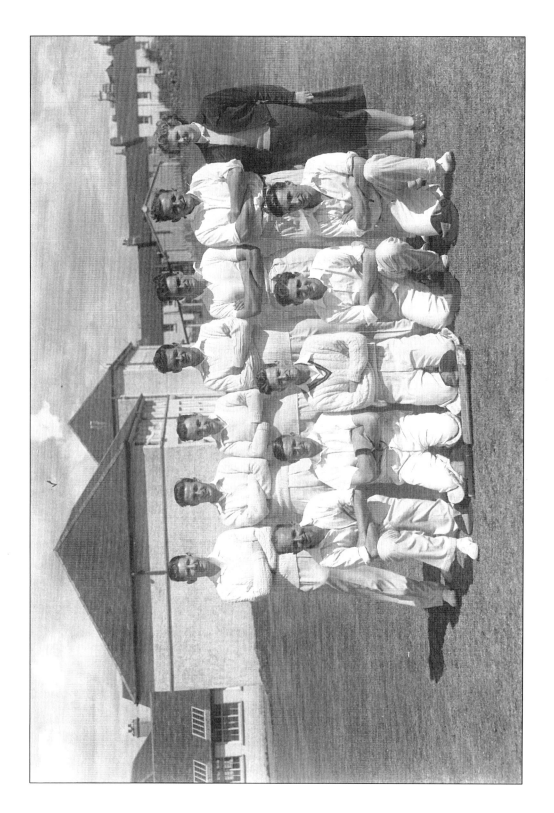

The Regatta also used to feature a major sports programme which was centred in the Sports Ground. Here from 1960 we see Chris Wood of the Bideford Amateur Athletics Club winning the 220 yards race in front of a large crowd in the old grandstand.

Above: This shot from September 1965 records a visit by Barnstaple to play Bideford in an F.A.Cup qualifying match. The two Bideford players are right-half Frank Meadows on the right and centre-half Brian Lancaster seen heading the ball away from the goal mouth.

Previous page: Honestone Street doesn't figure in many old photographs but here is one from 26 December 1968 which also features, rather oddly, a local hunt riding up the road. Just behind the fifth rider is the old Salvation Army building that used to stand next to the Pannier Market.

Next page: Cycling was a major new 'craze' from the 1890s onward, when cheaper machines allowed many more to own their own cycles. Service providers soon started to cater to the new hobbyists as this photograph taken outside what is today's 'Mr.Chips' on the Quay around 1900 shows.

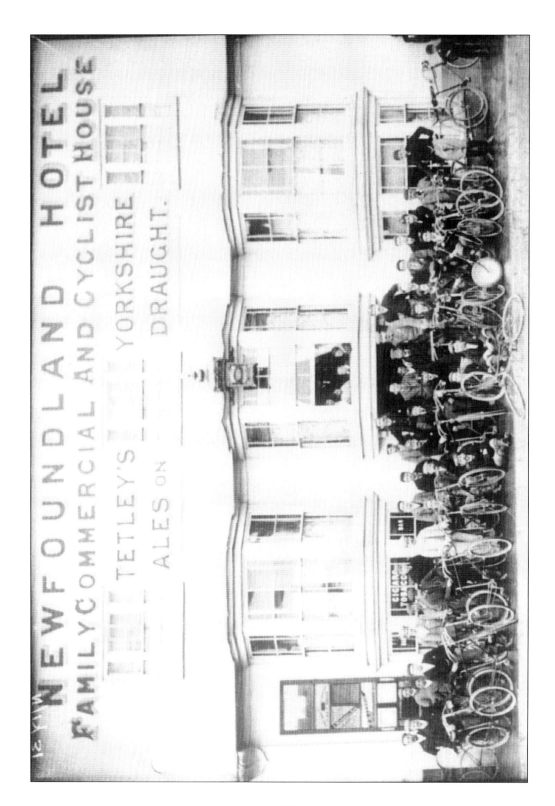

Miscellaneous

Above: The Quay was the natural focus for public events and here is one from the late 1920s or early 1930s – though what it is I am unable to say. Notice that nearly everyone is wearing a hat – and how flimsy looking is that push chair on the extreme left.

Next page: In my earlier books I have used various photographs of the Bideford Church Lads' Brigade and here is another. Its quasi-military set up is well shown with the uniforms, bugles and drums all prominent. The picture seems to have been taken at Saunton when the unit was on a camping trip just prior to the First World War.
Two more shots are from the same trip. Many local CLB members served in World War 1 – with some being killed or badly wounded.

Edgehill College was founded as a Bible Christian school for girls in 1884 and within a year had 42 pupils. It survived an outbreak of fever in 1887 and a devastating fire in 1920. This slightly damaged photograph shows the whole school body, both pupils and teachers around 1910.

In every volume of this series I have featured photographs from the archives of the Braddick family and here is another. Taken around the 1950s it shows their diminutive mobile loudspeaker van next to the Kingsley statue on a very deserted river bank.

Westcroft School is now some 54 years old but still looks modern. This picture was taken very near to its opening – a time when all young boys wore shorts and all girls seemed to wear white socks and sandals.

We always remember our teachers so it is said - so there must be many who recall his lady. She was Miss. E.M.Davies, head of the Bideford Church Junior School from 1940-64. She has in fact taught at both Geneva Junior and Senior Schools for 8 years before that – so her pupils must have run into thousands. She is pictured here in January 1964 just prior to retirement.

Above: The church clock in St.Mary's church tower was installed in 1878 and so, by 1966 when this photograph was taken was showing its age – so much so that it had broken down. The picture shows Douglas French on the left and Torrington clock-maker Arthur Dyer trying to get it going again.

Previous page: I have printed various photographs of the Bideford Sea Cadets in my books and here is another. Taken in July 1964 it shows cadets loading fuel on to T.S.*Revenge* before a fortnight's cruise to Ireland and the Welsh coast.

Next page: In the Summer of 1966 the Bideford Labour Party and the Young Socialists manned this caravan/café 24 hours a day along the A39 Bideford to Bude road to provide tea for weary travellers – in this refurbished caravan which they painted in the Labour party colours of red and yellow.

161

Above: Grenville College has recently combined with Edgehill College but here from March 1967 we see the headmaster John Crabbe laying the foundation stone of a new dormitory block at Moreton. Also laying stones were the Bishop of Crediton, the Archdeacon of Taunton, housemaster David Young, head prefect Ian Ferguson and head of School House Edward Pot.

Previous page: This photograph dates from March 1980 and shows a smiling group of young instrumentalists who were members of the Bideford School brass band. They had just won an audition at Exeter which allowed them to go forward to the National Festival of Music for Youth being held in Croydon in July of that year.

Next page: The Rotaract organisation is the youth wing of the Rotary Club which undertakes various good works. In January 1981 the Bideford Club put on a New Year's children's party at the New Inn in the town. They seem to be enjoying themselves – even given the rather overpowering wallpaper behind them!

Above: In Volume 2 I used a photograph showing the visit of Prince Charles to Bideford in February 1984. A lot of people said they recognised themselves or their children – so here is another one showing the Prince doing a 'walkabout' on the Bridge with the Royal Hotel in the background.

Previous page: The Bridge Trust is some 700 years old having been originally created to look after the Bridge. It gradually became a major charity even though many are unaware of just what it does as it does not court publicity. Here we see some of the Trustees presenting a specialised operating microscope to the Bideford Ear, Nose and Throat clinic in May 1985. From left to right the attendees were Dr.I.Hewetson (BBT), Dr.S.Richardson, Dr.J.Riddington Young (seated), Peter Trapnell (BBT), Miss Else (Chief Nursing Officer), H.Cleaver (BBT, seated), ?, Stan Short (BBT).

Next page: I have included this shot just to show that photographs do not have to be old to be interesting. It shows the long thin fields of Londonderry Farm before the estate that took its name was built. Taken in the early 1980s the white building in the centre is the sewage pumping station and above it are the houses of Slade.

Bideford's first troop of Boy Scouts was founded around 1910 being then known as Baden-Powell Scouts. Some of their very first members are shown in this picture which was taken soon after the troop started – when none had any badges to judge from their uniforms.

Another shot of the Scouts showing them exercising with small dumb-bells in front of an admiring audience. Fitness was, and still is, a major strand of Scouting.

For many years people living around the Kenwith Valley suffered from flooding whenever heavy rain coincided with high tides in the Torridge. Eventually the existing flood scheme with its dam, pumps and channels was put in place – and as part of it local groups planted trees in the area both to beautify it and to take up some of the excess water. Here we see the 1st. Torridge Cub Scouts of Northam planting saplings in March 1986.

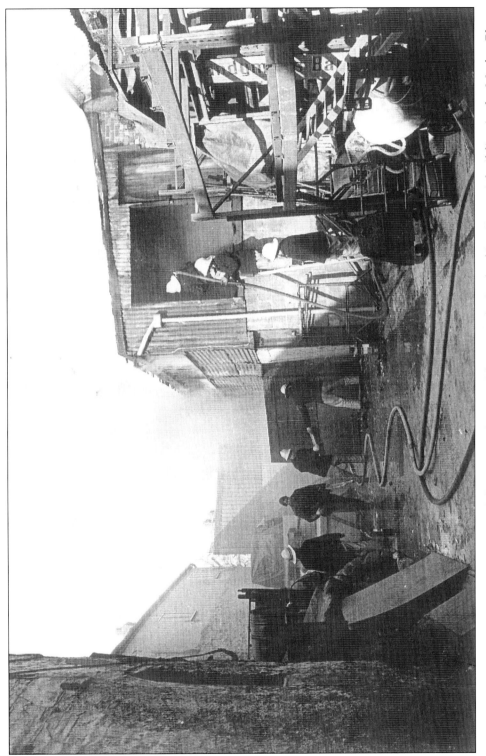

Fires in buildings are always dramatic and this action shot records one at the back of Jon Brown's building in the Market Place (in the yard of the old Angel Inn) in March 1986 with men from the Bideford Fire Brigade in attendance.

The decision to pedestrianise Mill Street for most of the day was a contentious one with shopkeepers, and some councillors, forecasting doom and gloom if it was done. Eventually, however, it was decided to go ahead and here in March 1988 we see a workman laying the paviors that were used to distinguish between the 'road' and 'pavement'. The old 'Gateway' supermarket is in the background.

The area of saltmarshes at East-the-Water have long attracted houseboats, which though not always looking very smart, have provided accommodation for those unable (or averse) to access normal housing. This shot dates from October 1988 and shows a rather chaotic scene with two of these vessels.

Notes

Notes

Lazarus Press
DEVON